The Unfastening

The Unfastening

Poems

Wesley McNair

DAVID R. GODINE · *Publisher*

BOSTON

First published in 2017 by
DAVID R. GODINE · *Publisher*
Post Office Box 450
Jaffrey, New Hampshire 03452
www.godine.com

LIBRARY OF CONGRESS CATALOGING-IN-PUBLICATION DATA

Names: McNair, Wesley, author.
Title: The unfastening / by Wesley McNair.
Description: Jaffrey, New Hampshire : David R. Godine, 2017.
Identifiers: LCCN 2016050105 | ISBN 9781567925999 (alk. paper) |
ISBN 1567925995
Classification: LCC PS3563.C388 A6 2017 | DDC 811/.54—dc23
LC record available at https://lccn.loc.gov/2016050105

FIRST EDITION
Printed in the United States

Contents

For Donald Hall
and
for Diane

1 · *The Unfastening*

The Button

It's not easy to button the top
button on the dress shirt
of an old man, his chin back,

his helpless hands
dangling at his sides
imagining themselves

doing what they're now
unable to do as you struggle,
close enough you share

his labored breath
and feel the growing
distance between what

he wants and cannot have,
and the distance
has become you,

not done with him and this
small, unyielding button,
even after you are done.

My Mother's Penmanship Lessons

In her last notes, when her hand began
to tremble, my mother tried to teach it

the penmanship she was known for,
how to make the slanted stems

of the p's and d's, the descending
roundness of the capital m's, the long

loops of the f's crossed at the center,
sending it back again and again

until each message was the same:
a record of her insistence that the hand

return her to the way she was before,
and of all the ways the hand had disobeyed.

Nursing Home Haikus

A decorative
front door, the back rehabbed for
anything on wheels.

With each step, the right
foot finds the floor for the left
foot, which cannot feel.

When guests come he looks
up, then down for the open
place in his darkness.

It stops at each door:
an ice-cream truck with no bell,
just pills, a clipboard.

Right then, waving them
off, smiling, she was having
her last heart attack.

Are you going? When
are you going? When are you
going to come back?

Once this whole floor was
the ballroom of a mansion.
Think of the rooms cleared

away for dancing,
the gowns, the music that said
now, and only now.

The Afterlife

After my mother's dying, after
the nurses turned her stiff body
toward me in her bed so I heard
up close the lengthening pauses

of her breathing, after even the hand
I held went slack, and her eyes opened wide
and sightless forever, I wandered
through the high, dead grasses,

past the broken spine of the house
she would not leave, and past
the overgrown shrubs and the raised
beds of weeds, to the nursery barn

she hadn't entered for months,
except in her mind. In that twilight,
flakes of the first snow came out
of the wind like fireflies, and ancient

stained rags of canvas swayed
in the doorway. Where I was was
not there, yet there, not the living place
she remembered over and over,

but also dying, everything inside
releasing itself from the dreamlife
of her longing: up-ended greenhouse
windows, sprung garden rakes, chicken wire,

a mulching machine that no longer mulched
listing on two flat tires. Above my head
in a heaven of old, forgotten chains
nailed to the wall, a rigid choir

of potted plants hung on a wire,
and a hole in the roof which couldn't
care less kept letting down snow
on the love seat my mother

and stepfather never sat in,
and his defunct rototiller, and the tools
on the shelf not stolen by the hired men,
who, year after year, reminded her of him.

Nobody was there to find it all
together reclaiming itself in the late light
as the given up and given out
but me, also returning from the sorrow

of her dreamlife, stunned by the clarity
of what it wasn't, and what it was.

When They Lay Down

They didn't close their eyes when they lay down
As if getting ready for a long night's sleep.
My old, truant father rose for work hung over.
My mother gardened in the dark with a headlamp.

As if getting ready for a long night's sleep,
My stepfather lay under his jacked-up car.
My mother gardened in the dark with a headlamp.
At the end, my parents were so tired.

My stepfather lay under his jacked-up car
When it suddenly gave way and came down on him.
At the end, my parents were so tired.
Some days, my father forgot his socks;

Then it all gave way and came down on him.
On his knees in my dream, my father tries to speak.
Some days, he even forgot his socks.
My mother couldn't feel her whole left side.

On his knees in my dream, my father tries to speak.
He rose for work every day hung over.
My mother couldn't feel her whole left side.
They didn't close their eyes when they lay down.

I Praise My Mother, the House Lover, at Last

who came through the sudden death of my stepfather
    and the fire from the wood stove, ready
      to love the house as she never had before;

who went to the dumpster after the workmen left to carry
    the blistered chairs, and the books, swollen
      by fire hoses, and the childhood dresses of her grown
      daughter – all back to the house where they belonged;

who carefully saved each newspaper and magazine
    and circular and unopened bill addressed to it;

who walked through the stacks of them, and the bags
    of clothes and empty cans, and the disused lamps
      and flowerpots, armed only with her cane;

who kept her door closed to anyone who didn't understand
    her daily, thoughtful housekeeping, speaking in a firm
      voice to neighbors, home-health nurses, tax assessors,
      and me through the screen of her bathroom window;

who imagined a family to bring into the house, handymen
    just like her husband, and a gardener, more like
      her daughter, she said, than her real daughter;

who never noticed the work left undone as she wandered
    with them in the yard, past the collapsing fence,
      and the buckling outbuildings, and the gardens
      where morning glories and vetch bloomed;

who, loving the house with her whole mind, did not see how
      bereft it looked with its cracked walk and dipping roof;

who ignored the wishes of the doctors in acute care
      and returned to live among the pathways inside
      her house just as it was, her greatest wish;

who called for it from her bed in her small, shared room
      at the nursing home with a longing so deep, I felt
      the blow of each stroke that undid her love for it.

Clem's Stroke

A silent lightning
cracked him
in two, one leg
dangling a foot

that can't feel
the floor
when he walks,
the other guiding it,

a zig-zag dance,
and he the impresario
with his cane.
My Uncle Clem,

the military man
once so tucked in
nobody
could dig him out,

now unable
to tuck himself,
or trust his slack
tongue with only

what he wants it
to say. Yet see
him smile
with bunny teeth

when he whispers
to the new girlfriend
he sits beside,
and the feeling

that rises into
his fingers as he not
quite touches
her white hair,

arriving despite himself
out in the open,
his little death
bringing him to life.

The Unfastening

As the father turns away from the thought
of his failure, the hands remove
his glasses and rub his eyes over

and over, drying the nonexistent tears.
Unknown to the one who is troubled
about losing his hair, his fingers stroke

his baldness as he speaks. The body,
our constant companion, understands
the loneliness of the hostess in her dark

driveway, embracing herself after the guests
who promised *more* and *soon* have gone,
and even visits the old schoolteacher

who reads the same happy ending to each
new class, working her toes in her shoes.
How could the people of the kingdom

not have known the curse of sorrow
was nothing more than a long sleep
they had only to wake from? In dreams

the body, which longs for transformation
too, suddenly lifts us above the dark
roofs of our houses, and far above

the streets of the town, until they seem
like any other small things fastened to earth.

2 · *The Master of Loss*

The Fun of Running Back and Forth

Running back and forth from the living room
to the kitchen of that small apartment
with my younger brother, carrying magazines,
is my first memory of having fun, rolling them up

tight in the way I invented and showed him,
since the idea was to sneak up behind
our father and spank him, each of us shrieking
with delight when we made him reach out

to us, turning away from our mother
with her head bowed over the dishpan,
and when he went back to his shouting, we ran
for more magazines to surprise my father,

who had never shouted, but did now
because she wouldn't stop suspecting his lie,
his betrayal, which my brother and I, just three
and four, knew nothing about then, only

wanting to keep on laughing about the fun
of forcing our father, who would leave
again soon, this time for good,
to turn back and reach out to us,

so our mother would not go on
with her crying anymore, and make us cry.

My Brother's Paper Route

Now that the route was mine,
I could buy a new bike like his,
I thought, and imagined how I looked
as I climbed uphill wearing the bag,

a kind of uniform, with its broad
orange band crossing my chest.
Nobody watched from the windows
except the old woman in a bathrobe

who called me into her dim room
to sit with her while she spread
her newspaper out on the table,
pulling the small letters under

the pool of her magnifying glass.
When she let me out at last
in the twilight, the houses were gone
to shadow. Was this the apartment

my brother had shown me in the peeling
triple-decker? Was this the right
triple-decker? The man inside
who shouted at his wife wouldn't

come to the door. And what was I to do
under the streetlamp about the three
leftover newspapers in my bag
and the ache in my shoulder

from carrying it, too young to understand
the poverty and loneliness on that hill
of streets, or how what you thought
you owned could own you.

Delight

What did the milk know
when my youngest spilled it
from a cup all those mealtimes
except to follow the long slant

of our table that led to my lap,
and what did the four
children know when I rose
to invoke the name of our Lord,

except to laugh, then laugh
because they shouldn't, and how
could my son, the lover of books,
who crawled under our new

mattress to discover a curtained
chamber, read to himself without
lighting the candle? He was no less
surprised than I was, waking up

from my nap and smelling smoke,
that he'd set the box-springs
on fire, and when my two oldest
gazed, as if for the first time,

at the topmost windows
of our rented barn feeling
an itch in their fingers for stones
small enough to fly,

what were they to do but search
for them? It was only delight
that called their attention
to the milk that jogged past

their plates down our table,
and to the candle that lit up
the chamber, and to the sharp,
winged stones, and when I

warned them or chased them
or drew them toward me for my
explanations, it was only delight
I wanted myself, my lessons

breaking into shouts, my spent
lungs struggling for breath.

The Human Creature

All you have to do
to see how close we are
to creatures who do not frown
in silence while writing words

is to observe a man holding
his fingers awkwardly
around a pen as he drags it
across the page.

All you have to do to realize
how troublesome it is
to be a human being dressed up
is watch a man keep

tucking in his shirt
which the body pushes
out of his pants as he walks,
or look at his misshapen shoes

kicked over beside the bed
as he lies fast asleep.
Entering his dream
of himself as a creature

without his clothes
is all you have to do to know
his loneliness, walking into room
after room where no one

understands him, trying
to cover himself with his hands.

Is It Begging - This?

Is it begging, this
impatient chin on your chair's
arm, or a question

about who you are,
a haired creature like him, yet
sitting with papers

or staring across
the room at a large, lit screen
with no smell at all.

Not now, you tell him,
but now's what sends him to you
with his alert ears

that seem to listen
to what you don't say, before
he closes himself

inside the circle
he makes for his dream. Is it
you he cries for there

by your chair, his legs
now quickening, returning
him to his senses?

Russell in the Road

Whenever the revolution breaks out
in this country, he's ready to go, dressed
in camouflage all the way up to the visor
on his cap, but today outside the town store,
fast-talking with his lips close together

to hold in his upper plate, Russell doesn't
rant about how the government is taking away
our freedom, or the surprise the terrorists
are in for if they show up in his front yard,
but the neighbor who shot his deer, the doe

he'd been making friends with all summer.
Has he always talked to deer, or did it start after
his kids left and his wife of forty years moved
out on him?– first to the doe, then to the little
faun she left behind, going down on his haunches

right there beside the gas pumps to show how
he walked toward it, whispering to coax it
out of the road and into the woods beyond.
Russell isn't in the road when I drive to the dump
past his lonely scarecrow and his house like a bunker

with high windows nobody can look into,
but I think of him, no taller than a faun himself
as he squats down and walks, trying to find
the words for the danger that lurks all around
the two of them, and the need for safety.

The Rhubarb Route

On a spring evening in between the black fly season
and the first mosquitoes, as the red stems lift
their broad leaves like scores of tilted umbrellas,
I call them on the telephone of my mind and drive
bagfuls of rhubarb down through the town, past
the white revenants of the Grange Hall and the closed
library, past the house lots and the treeless modulars
where they have no use for rhubarb, turning at last into
a wide driveway while little Herman, alive as anyone,
comes out of his old farmhouse with his chesty walk
to take two bags inside to Faye, enough for a whole
year of pies and red jello cobblers, then drive the back
way along the river, by the oaks and sumacs gathering
the shadows of twilight, to swing in beside the dead
school bus of True's cowless farm and see old Billy,
before his legs gave out, who loved rhubarb almost
as much as his long-lost mother, take the biggest bag
of it into his arms and carry it up the steps of his porch,
leaning on the rail to wave goodbye. Goodbye to Billy,
goodbye to little Herman, goodbye to the Gagnons,
who laugh in the deepening dusk about eating sticks
of rhubarb right from the patch as kids, goodbye
to my old neighbor Ethlyn in the house on the corner,
empty for two years, who all the same calls out
Hello from somewhere inside when I knock, *Hello,*
I'm here, and suddenly she is here next to me behind
the screen, smiling because I've remembered her again
on this spring evening with fresh rhubarb, which
she holds up to her face, breathing it in with a long
breath, before she turns and goes back into the dark.

This Poem

Before the age of doing
and photographing and filming
and texting what you did,
back when people simply did,
a girl got married at seventeen,

recalled tonight under lamplight
in an Ozark farmhouse by my old,
widowed Aunt Dot, the woman
who once was her. There were no
photos of the girl as she waited

in the truck with her first
two babies for her husband
to come out of the bar
until it was dark, and then
in the dark. Nobody filmed him

at the screen door of the kitchen,
waking from the spell
of his anger with a lead pipe
in his hand saying, "I believe
I killed that cow," or filmed her

stepping between his fists
and her son on the night he broke
her nose. Literal, plainspoken
and sorrowful, Dot seems
to find her, the poor young girl,

married for life, and him, my uncle,
the good old boy everyone loved,
including me, in the shadows
cast by her lamp and chair,
just the three of them there,

and me, and the small,
hand-held device of this poem.

Kay

Everybody in the family knew the story
of how Henry's war bride got out of the car
in the yard dressed up in a kimono
and bowing. Their father was so surprised
he dropped his pail of feed. None of them
ever wondered about the shock she
must have felt to find her new father-in-law
among a gang of hogs in the Ozarks
wearing bib overalls and a straw hat.
She being a foreigner, it was *her* job
to understand *him*. "Over there," Henry said,
they eat fish raw," and he had his older
sister show her how to make biscuits
and pork gravy. In the end, sorrow opened them
to her. After just seven years, Henry,
who'd been drinking, drove his truck over
an embankment and died in the accident,
leaving her with two young girls, and hardly able
to speak English. Henry's brother got her a job
as a waitress at the local restaurant, and his sisters
took turns babysitting. "You could eat right
off her floors," one of them told a friend,
and later, when the restaurant's owner
promoted her to bookkeeper, they bragged
about how fast her fingers moved on the abacus
she'd brought from Japan. There, no one
would have understood how her first daughter,
who looked like Henry except for her black hair
and her eyes, could have been so wild
as to jump on a motorcycle at fifteen behind

her new boyfriend, and her mother couldn't make
herself understand it, either. "Oh, Kay,"
the women said at the funeral, holding her,
for by then she was part of the family.
None of them ever wondered about her real
name, or knew how pleased she was long before
to have this one, which Henry gave her
on the way to America, where she would spend
the rest of her life discovering who Kay was.

The Master of Loss

My old Uncle Truman, a career military man
used to being in charge, was the first of us inside
my mother's house, followed by Bonnie,
the high-school sweetheart he'd returned to
in the Ozarks after the sudden death of his wife,
next, his Ozark sister Dot and brother Wallace,

then me. We didn't visit the greenhouse with its torn
plastic ceiling and desiccated plants on the table
and hoses on the floor tangled in pots and coffee cans.
Yet the house was all my aunt needed to have nightmares
for two weeks afterward, shocked that whenever her older
sister called her long distance from New Hampshire

late at night, telling her stories about the workers
at her nursery and big sales of the forsythia my dead
stepfather once developed, she sat at a desk surrounded
by piles of old bills and newspapers, or worse,
in the bathroom on the toilet seat's matted, black fur
talking on the portable phone among magazines scattered

all over the floor. "How can she live like this?" Dot asked,
because everyone understood you had to keep things
in their proper places to know where they were.
But here, my stepfather's overalls and shirts,
which belonged in the closet, were hanging on the bar
of the shower stall, and his shoes were beneath them

in the unwashed tub, and the floor was such a mess
neither she, unsteady on her swollen legs, nor Truman,
on his cane, dared venture beyond the door frame.

Back in the living room, I found Wallace, who wore
a wide bandage across his bald head, searching
through the bookshelf for the family bible my mother

accused him of stealing after my grandmother's
funeral, having forgotten that she took it herself.
"Ten to one, it burned up in the fire she had," he said
with a sigh, probably because now he couldn't
carry it back to the rehab hospital and show it to her
as he smiled the same smile that my grandmother

couldn't resist in her youngest son, and that my mother
always hated, thinking of all he got away with
when he was a child, and he, remembering all
she used to blame him for. Yet there was plenty here
for him to gloat about. In the kitchen with Bonnie,
Truman tried the faucet over the sink, which chugged,

then blasted black water on the encrusted pans
in the sink. "My God, they's a big mouse trap in between
the cans on the floor!" Dot exclaimed. Truman shut
the faucet off hard with a scowl, more upset
than she was, for after living his whole life by rules
and order, he must have felt he was now standing

in disorder itself. "She's lost her grip for sure," he said,
the faucet still fast in his hand, and we others agreed,
because for each of us, life had to do with holding on,
however you managed it, against surprises and losses,
Truman returning to the past with his high-school
sweetheart, Aunt Dot, disoriented unless she knew

where things belonged, Uncle Wallace, distracted
for now from his growing cancer by a family grudge,
and I myself, who in my grief for a failing mother
had brought these dear, diminished siblings
from their visit at the hospital to see the stacks
and piles and pathways as if the house were a problem

that somehow we could fix. Bent to our purposes,
we missed the message right there around us,
that even as we held on by turning away from loss,
my old, exasperating mother, grown tired
of turning away, had reached out to embrace it, holding
onto everything she had so tightly it could never leave.

3 · *The Longing To See*

My Stepfather's Cars

When my stepfather returned
from the machine shop, all
he wanted to do was get under
the hood or chassis of a junked car
in his backyard, trying, against
the odds to fix it with parts
taken from other cars and failing
over and over. What did it all
come to? Where was the world,
and where was poetry? I couldn't
wait to get away from that house
far from town, yet now, an old man,
I see that I never left it, living
apart from others while I work
each day on a poem, raiding
junked drafts for parts and trying
against the odds to make it run.

Old Poets

At the literary luncheon for the old poet
in lace, her gray-haired daughter is still
hurt by her mother's attachment
to the book. When the daughter
asked what was for supper as a girl,
she tells the others, her mother
went on typing up the manuscript
while reciting with a smile a tiny,
ironic poem: "Air soup and wind
pudding." The poet refuses to believe it,
and denies chasing her daughter
all over the house with a shoe brush
for neglecting to mail the finished
manuscript at the post office.
For what mother would make such a cruel
choice between her two children?

*

At the end, when he wore
the address and photograph
of his own house around his neck,
his wife and son always
knew where to find him:
at the town grocery, inviting
the women who came in
to dance. After a lifetime
of going to his upstairs study
to write the poems critics praised
for pushing feeling away

into his carefully assigned ellipses
and margins, he couldn't stop
reaching for this rhythm
of the body, this joyful embrace.

*

After he told his friends in sadness
the poetry had stopped, he discovered
on his computer the beautiful poems
he once abandoned, staying up
for a whole night in the excitement
of finishing them. This was the way
he began again, learning through his own
failures how the despair of giving up
can open the heart to poetry.

*

At the public celebration of his birthday,
he waved to his audience
from the stage, modest and fragile.
In his email to a friend he was the old
warrior: "Fuck 87! All month
the writing has been going crap."

*

Shocked by her exhaustion
as she suddenly turned and fell

straight down on the bed
in her writing room, I missed
until this moment the whole show:
her impatience with her body's
slow walk toward the desk
to show me her new book,
the pure determination of her hard
fist as she lifted herself over
and over on her cane until
at last she held the collection,
forgetting in her smile of triumph
her old bones and all the failed
drafts of her struggle to place it
in my hands. And then she fell.

Stephen Ash's Invitation

The proud sea captain who built it
decades before, the grandest house of all
the islands, never imagined a man
like Stephen Ash would one day inherit it,
painting the exposed lath on the ceilings
with bright colors and writing mottos
about life and art right on the walls

of the stairwell. We pass by them
on the way up, pass the bedroom
of his overbearing, practical father, asleep
in the gravesite down the street, to linger
in the room where Stephen once stretched
canvases for the old woman who long ago
rented it, telling him with a raised finger

like his to me as he stands, nearly
to the top of the doorframe, in old, cracked
shoes, his pant-cuffs rolled up, buttons
forgotten on his shirt: "Look around you,
Stevie, gather the truth in your eye."
Sixty years later, his own attempts at art
have taken over each dusty, faded

landing we come to: distant, lit strands
with trees, odd angles of ocean and sky,
paintings finished and unfinished,
his kind of housekeeping after being kept
by other houses all his life, sealed up
window and door. Now, in the grand ruin
of this house become his ruin, he leads me

to the final stairway, below an opening
so bright it leaves the two of us almost
in darkness, its light, his light. Above us
as I climb behind him, the sound of the wind
that blew away the last rail of the widow's
walk last winter grows in our ears, but
never mind, he says, on the windiest days

he ties the rope cinched there to the rafter
around his waist so he won't blow
away, too. And suddenly Stephen's outside
on the roof so I can stand on the top step,
with him in the wind and light. Far off,
beyond the town's settled streets and rows
of gravestones, the shimmering islands,

large and small, break free from the land,
their wild, beautiful trees floating as if
on air all the way to the horizon. "Look,"
is all he says, oddly calm with his flying
white hair and his smile that is not mad
exactly. Then I stand out on the roof
beside him as the two of us gather it in.

My Mother's Harvest Centerpiece

Out of the space of supper plates
pushed back, out of her all-night falling asleep
and waking up to arrange it on the tray

under the hanging lamp, this perfect, twined
circle of twigs and autumn leaves she collected
from the dirt driveway of our tarpapered
garage-house. Out of the next day's forgotten

breakfast and lunch – no appetite now
but for making it – this cardboard wish
of a house with a picture window, floating

on the soft, unseasonable green
of Easter grass, with longer tufts of grass
on each side of the front door, wide open
to let out a long line of pipe-cleaner kids,

enough to make the women who'll view them
tonight at the square dance club dinner laugh.
Under her smile as she thinks of their laughter

and turns the small world she constructs like a god
to glue on the kids' paper dresses and pants,
the sorrow of her own childhood
raising six younger siblings in the Ozarks,

and pregnant now herself for the fourth time.
Underneath the mother she has made
at the center of the centerpiece –

a faceless clothespin woman that the children
converge upon – who else but herself,
her endless chores on my stepfather's would-be
farm like the woman's impossible chore

of feeding with no hands a flock of jurassic
plastic chickens, nearly as tall as she is?
Underneath this clothespin farmer leaning

toward the woman with no way to touch her,
who but my stepfather, the man now pacing
in the twilight and shouting that she's taken so
damn long with the centerpiece, the dinner

is going to start without it? Out of the deep dream
my mother goes right on dreaming, the wide
outer circle of vegetables from our family's unhappy

harvest in the back field: turnips and baby winter
squashes and potatoes like gloomy hills
the little family can't see beyond. From her old
grudges as a wife and the fights of her father

and mother, from her life as the oldest child
far from town in the Ozarks, a pipe-cleaner girl
set apart, waving with a hole in her hand.

The Longing To See

You won't be able
to see through it,
said the surgeon who
put the dark bubble

of gas into my sick
eye, yet if I held it
just so, I could steal
inside its small,

refracted world,
broken into beautiful
colors that sickness
and dark had made,

a sort of poetry
without the words,
which I returned to
even after the bubble

was gone -- all well
except for my old
incompleteness
and the longing

for its way of seeing,
the irresistible
looking out
while looking in.

The Poem

In the apparent
vacancy beyond
each line, you might
sense the poem

waiting to think
itself. Imagine
the surface of a twilight
pond in wind,

shifting and changing
the sky, then
going still
as a concentrating mind,

the far trees
deepening
in its reflection.
Like the poem

the pond's alive --
its beauty (the sudden
scintillation of a hundred
thousand wavelets)

and music (the percussion
of a beaver's tail)
arising from what is.
And when the pond

accumulates
the darkness,
which it loves,
it challenges your eyes

to find the light
that without darkness
you could not see.
Wild campsites

you never noticed
now appear
along the far shore.
It's not only itself

the poem waits for
moving line by line
into its own dark.
It waits for you.

4 · *Maintaining*

Losses

It must be difficult for God, listening
to our voices come up through his floor
of cloud to tell Him what's been taken away:
Lord, I've lost my dog, my period, my hair,
all my money. What can He say, given
we're so incomplete we can't stop being
surprised by our condition, while He
is completeness itself? Or is God more
like us, made in His image – shaking His head
because He can't be expected to keep track
of which voice goes with what name and address,
He being just one God. Either way, we seem
to be left here to discover our losses, everything
from car keys to larger items we can't search
our pockets for, destined to face them
on our own. Even though the dentist gives us
music to listen to and the assistant looks down
with her lovely smile, it's still our tooth
he yanks out, leaving a soft spot we ponder
with our tongue for days. Left to ourselves,
we always go over and over what's missing –
tooth, dog, money, self-control, and even losses
as troubling as the absence the widower can't stop
reaching for on the other side of his bed a year
later. Then one odd afternoon, watching something
as common as the way light from the window
lingers over a vase on the table, or how the leaves
on his backyard tree change colors all at once
in a quick wind, he begins to feel a lightness,
as if all his loss has led to finding just this.

Only God knows where the feeling came from,
or maybe God's not some knower off on a cloud,
but there in the eye, which tears up now
at the strangest moments, over the smallest things.

Imperfection

They're not imperfect,
exactly, just exact
in the wrong places,
the old, long-haired

dog with fuzz
on top of his head
and the young blond one
wearing an elegant

mustache of black skin
under her unusually
broad nose. She likes
to breathe through it

while mashing it against
her rump to bite a flea,
or stand on his upside-
down face biting his ears,

or pass him on her way
to bed up the stairs,
for him a mountain
of pain. He climbs up

sideways on his bad leg,
lifting it outdoors
next morning as high
as he can to pee

on her pee. Whatever,
she seems to say, off
rolling in whatever it was
overnight that died,

or maybe chasing her short
bent tail, disappearing
behind her except
for a feather of hair. His tail's

short too, so waiting for me
at the door, she with the bent
wag, he with the small,
jiggling fountain of fur,

even their sweet mutt joy's
imperfect, not exactly
the dogs I imagined when
they were pups, just them.

Love

Smoking outside the store
with the trucker, who's used
to being right, Stanley, the shy
clerk on break, agrees with him
that his doctors don't know
a damn thing, then moves
toward him, almost touching
his back, while the trucker,
his ragged beard shaking
with the effort, tries to reach
a tightness in his lungs
with his shallow cough.

*

"Love" is not the sort of word you'd expect
from a man wearing a camo jacket and boots
who keeps his hunting dogs in a pen outdoors
so they won't get spoiled, and an outdoors
man himself. But tonight under the lamplight,
he's one week into a fishing trip with nothing
to do but tell the others about the house-dog
his wife at home talked him into, and how else
to explain without that word, why the dog can't
stop whining whenever she's away, and follows
her all over the house like a damn fool?

*

Just after Francis, age 90, asks
the customer at his apple orchard
in his loud voice what to do now
that his watchdog has gone
deaf, too, the dog shows up
in the driveway with his matted fur
and one gray eye, delighted to find
his master there and lick his hand.

*

The substitute minister, far off
at the pulpit, asks who's new today
in church, then raises his own hand.
Nobody laughs. It's his voice
that dazes them, a breezy, lighthearted
tone for a joke, a caring tone
for sympathizing with their needs,
a helpless tone for asking Christ,
in his everlasting love, to assist them.
Up close after the service,
as they shake his hand and look into
his evasive eye, they see the voice
is how he protects himself from them.

*

All through this November day
of troubles, when I reach unthinking
into my pants pocket and touch

the damp bills, I remember her,
the quiet one with the bruised skin
under her eyes from no sleep,
dumping out my wet empties
in the town redemption center
with her young, gloveless hands,
as downcast in that dim room as I was.
Still she went on counting one
by one, in a rhythm that grew like
a faithful, intimate song between us
until, pausing to wipe her palms
and press the bills into my hand,
she smiled a big smile, the shock of it
seeming to lift me, lift us both, up
over the broken-down boxes and plastic
bags of used-up bottles and cans.

What I Remember

The voice of the sweet woman who came
from across the road, telling me
you were sitting right beside her,
then handing you her cell phone.

My panic as I searched for you
in the dark afterward, rounding the turn
you missed to discover the blue
hysterics of the police lights.

The ambulance's room, oddly quiet,
where you looked up under blankets
to assure me you were fine, though
you had never seemed so fragile.

The forgotten kitchen chair I passed
on the way back to my car
to follow you, which the woman
must have carried to the road's edge

so you could sit with the phone,
asking my name over and over,
as if you couldn't believe
it belonged to you.

Getting Lost

I'm not proud of it, but I couldn't resist
Serena, the British woman on my GPS,
who understood I had better things to do
while driving than to think about what
I was doing, and who had the most charming

difficulty with her r's. I went everywhere
with her, making each turn she whispered
with that lisp of hers into my ear as I watched
the man she had made of me on my GPS TV,
a superhero in a blue car taking on the tangle

of roads that tumbled out of the horizon,
until Diane, my wife and former navigator,
who couldn't match Serena's expertise,
not to mention her modest compliance, began
to resent her. "She says 'rump' instead of 'ramp,'"

Diane remarked as I made another perfect
exit off the thruway, "and that thing she does
with her r's is driving me nuts." It was wonderful
to be the source of conflict between two
women, but then I began to consider how

my destination time in the lower left corner
kept adjusting itself according to my speed,
a small reminder that in the very moment
I was enjoying my triumph over the map,
a computer somewhere that knew everything

was mapping me. I recall a certain period
of melancholy before I returned to my wife,
Serena and I had been that good together,
I having made so many wrong turns
in my life, she only wanting to help me

make them right. Yet I couldn't stop longing for,
of all things, the fights Diane and I once had
about the urgency of finding our way,
and the seductive thought of ending up
beside some forgotten field among cows

on a dwindling road that didn't even exist
on the ragged copy of the known world
she held in her lap. Which was, minus the cows,
just where we were one week after I unplugged
the GPS, and we sat quietly at the roadside

spent by our argument, she turning to me
with her blue eyes and that old, dear expression
of helplessness, I falling in love all over again
because there was no Serena to recalculate,
only the two of us together once more, getting lost.

The Revolution

for Kathleen

On a day in this post-9/11 nation,
where our cars are protected
by sensors and cameras
and black glass that keeps us safe

from the sun and each other,
my daughter-in-law drove me
and her kids down the main street
of Felton, California, in an SUV
that wore brand new, long

eyelashes over its headlights.
The tinted glass of parked vans
refused our reflection. A pickup
with window guards, and cars

with squinting, watchful headlights
passed by before we turned
into the parking lot of the school.
But on this day of the eyelashes,
which transformed her SUV

into a human face, the face
of a woman, mothers we didn't
recognize honked their horns,
putting up their thumbs,

and when the black glass
of the SUV's and the mini-vans

opened, other moms came out
with their kids to gather around us
in intimacy and wonder. "I love

the lashes," one woman said,
clutching her heart and laughing.
"Where can we get a pair?"
somebody else wanted to know,

the start of a small revolution
to free us from the protections
of Homeland America.

Maintaining

Don't think you know the fat woman
in charge of the dump, married
to the one laid up from the accident
two years ago at the pulp mill,
who wears the easygoing, happy
face when you drive in with your load
of trash, calling her name. That's not her.

*

By the register at the store, truckers,
carpenters and mill workers
count their change while telling
the morning clerk how they are:
"Not too bad." "Could be worse."
"Maintaining."

*

Billy Towle maintains. His mother,
he explains after bush-hogging my field,
has come down with All-timers,
and begun calling him by his dead
father's name. He shakes his head:
a sad situation, but even so,
you can see he kind of likes it,
perhaps because in the All-time
of her mind, his father, whose death
she mourned for years, can still be alive.
Also because now, the one he's always
loved most will always love him.

*

People here don't talk much
about love. Listen for it
in other words – how old
Ethelyn Palmer lingers slightly
over the word "grandchildren,"
or describes her new neighbors
with what seems a fond
description of her own past
in this town: "They're a young
couple, just starting out."

*

And just because they don't speak
of beauty doesn't mean they haven't
noticed it: the sunset's astonishment
of red on the horizon, tinting the town's
downhill windows, for instance, or how
at night, in your headlights as you travel
the last mile home, the feathery pines
alongside your car seem to gather
you up in the wings of their dark flight.

*

But what of the stranger at town meeting
with the designer suit and perfect
manners, sympathetic to everyone's

questions about his proposal to turn
LeFlamme's back field into house lots
because he knows his audience can't refuse?
"I would urge you to consider the large
increase in your tax base," he says.

*

Twelve years later his faded
sign with the lot map announces
MyPropertyForYou.com
to the ivy dangling from it
and the vestiges of a gravel road
curving alongside power poles.
In the enclosure of pines his men
planted around lot 3, indentations
in the grass show where
the deer slept. Swallows rest
on the unused electric wire
off lots 6 and 7. And deeper still,
by the culverts where my dogs run,
waves of daisies, buttercups,
Indian paintbrushes and Queen
Anne's lace crest in the light wind,
more wildflowers than in any
year before. "Change doesn't need
to be a bad thing," he said.

*

Established by vanished farmers,
the Grange Hall's now
a ceramics studio. The old school,
bought for one dollar, houses
the town office, zumba classes,
and Story Time for kids.
A single-door rescue trailer
with a giant American flag decal,
obtained after the scare of 9/11
by a grant from Homeland Security,
rusts in the back. Having survived
the Industrial Revolution,
the regional school movement
and the rise of global terrorism,
our town's still here.

Telephone Poles

Like our cars, which have our faces,
and our houses, which look down
on us under their folded hats,

these resemble us, though nothing
we have made seems so steadfast.
Exiled to the roadside,

they stand in all weather, ignored
except for the rows of swallows
that remember them in springtime,

and the occasional tree holding up
a hole workmen have cut
to let the lines through. Yet they go on

balancing cables on their shoulders
and passing them to the next
and the next, this one extending

a wire to a farmhouse, that one
at the corner sending lines
four ways at once, until miles

away where the road widens,
and the tallest poles rise,
bearing streetlamps high above

the doors of the town, arriving
by going nowhere at all, each,
like the others that brought them here,

making its way by accepting
what's given, and holding on,
and standing still.

The Birthday Party

It was that time when your Uncle Rob was living
with your mother to help her out, do you remember?
When we arrived, the two of them were sitting
in their recliners like old marrieds, Rob, who always
liked dogs better than people, greeting not us,
but Woody, with all his heart. You walked straight
ahead with your tuna casserole to heat it up
in the kitchen while I followed carrying our bag
of gifts and the cake in my arms, past the new first-
floor bathroom with the white toilet seat as high
as my cake box. Herman had been dead for years,
of course, but he was all around us in the dining room
by way of his colored photographs of the camp
and the White Mountains that seemed to shimmer
in the August light. I remember the smell of the hot
rolls on the table and your casserole, its cheese
bubbling up into the breadcrumbs. Beside you
on her pillow wearing the napkin you tucked under
her chin, your mother looked a little like your child,
as in a sense she was. But when she told her story
about her older sister on the farm, still washing
her son's hair every week at age eighty-nine,
she was as funny as she always was. On that day,
Sue must have been – wasn't she? – eighty-three
herself, yet when you set the cake in front of her,
she blew out all eight candles and one to grow on
with a single breath. No way she was going to waste
her time with some wish about her uncertain future,
she called for the piece of cake she'd looked forward to
and dug right in. Meanwhile Rob, for his part, glanced

each way, then offered some of his cake to the dog
under the table, both of them assuming that the little
blessings of ordinary life as we all know them
would go on forever, no matter what. And they were right.

Praise Song

There was no stopping the old pear tree
in our backyard. After we released it
from a staked cord, it stood on the lawn
for a month as if coming to its decision
to lie back down on the ground again.
All winter we left it for dead, but in the spring
it lay in an island of unmowed grass
blooming beside its mate, and this May,
when I separate their branches
and look in, I find new shoots and flowers.

At the end of my life I want to lie down
in the long grass with one arm by my side
lifting me up as I reach out to her with all the others
and she reaches back. I want to know nothing
but the humming and fumbling of bees
carrying seed dust on their bellies from my blossoms
to her blossoms in the dome of green shade.

Benediction

Consider the lilies of the field,
how they grow
beyond their flowering, no longer
beautiful to our eyes. Consider
the brittle-petalled, black
centers of the black-eyed Susans,
waving like pom-poms
in the cold wind. There's a joy in it,
the joy of everything
that dances around it,
the milkweeds dangling their old,
goose-bumpy pods,
the Queen Anne's Lace
lifting the lacy purses
they have woven
from their blossoms. How could we
have overlooked the beauty
of the tiny, bristled stars
they now carry, or the hope,
among the brown clovers,
of the late bloomers, already living
the dream of their return?
Consider the dream
of the bloomers and of the wind-
torn blackberry bushes
holding out their stick fingers
that the birds have picked
clean. Consider the frosted heads
of the goldenrods

bending down to the ground,
and the milkweeds standing
straight up, giving themselves away.

About the Author

Wesley McNair has written nine volumes of poetry and two limited editions. He has also published a memoir, *The Words I Chose*, as well as books of prose and anthologies of Maine writing. A recipient of Guggenheim and Fulbright fellowships, he has received a United States Artists fellowship, two NEA grants, and two Rockefeller fellowships for creative work at the Bellagio Center in Italy. Other honors include the Theodore Roethke Prize, the Eunice Tietjens Prize from *Poetry* magazine, and an Emmy Award as scriptwriter for a series on Robert Frost that aired nationally on affiliates of PBS. His most recent book of poetry, *The Lost Child: Ozark Poems*, won the 2015 PEN New England Award for Literary Excellence in Poetry. He lives with his wife Diane in Mercer, Maine.

ACKNOWLEDGMENTS

Thanks to the following publications in which poems of this collection originally appeared, sometimes in different form: *Agni Review*, *American Life in Poetry*, *Cortland Review*, *Green Mountains Review*, *Journal of American Poetry*, *Innisfree Journal*, *Shenandoah*, and *Sewanee Review*. "Maintaining" was commissioned by the Community, Culture, and Conservation Conference at Colby College, April, 2016.

Special thanks to my editor, Chelsea Bingham, and to David Godine, whose ongoing faith in my work has made my career as a poet possible.

A NOTE ON THE TYPE

THE UNFASTENING *has been set in Ehrhardt, a type that first appeared in 1686 under the name "Holländsche Schriften" at the Ehrhardt type foundry in Leipzig. Clearly a cousin of the Janson types, it is likely that the type was cut by Nicolas Kis, a Hungarian punchcutter who worked in Amsterdam during the period 1680–89 and who is known to have left a set of matrices in Leipzig upon his return to Transylvania. Unlike the Janson types, though, Ehrhardt has less contrast between thick and thin strokes and has a narrower set width, features that give it a more even color on the page. The italic evinces a development toward more modern forms: The slopes of the letters are more consistent and the rhythm more regular than other italics of the same epoch. The slight condensation of both roman and italic makes Ehrhardt an elegant yet economical choice for text settings.*

DESIGN & COMPOSITION BY CARL W. SCARBROUGH